DECISIONS OF LIFE

FROM THE BOOK OF ESTHER

By

FAYE SAXON HORTON

Published in Fort Worth, Texas. Published by Horton International Ministries.

All inquiries should be addressed to:

Faye Saxon Horton

P O Box 8102

Ft Worth, TX 76124

hortoninternationalministries@gmail.com

This and other Horton International Ministries may be purchased in bulk for educational, business, Bible Study, fundraising, or sales promotions. For information email: hortoninternationalministries@gmail.com.

All Scripture references are New International Version, unless otherwise noted.

Print 2 – September, 2015

Dedications

Thanks to God for direction and guidance.

This book is dedicated to all the ladies closest to me; including family, friends, and all my associates. The women of BSF (Bible Study Fellowship) inspired me to continue to write. I offer special thanks and appreciation to BSF for your prayers and encouragement. To my sister, Janice, who read and re-read, reviewed and corrected; thanks for all your patience and help.

To my husband, Norris, who has endured hours of my being "on the computer". Your love and understanding allows me the freedom to write when the moment comes, while you do the cooking. Love you and thank you!

Thanks to each of you who have helped during the drafting stage, the beta stage, the testing stage, and the launching stage. Without your comments, guidance, time, patience and encouragements, putting this book out would have been difficult. You have made it easy for me to follow God's instructions. Thanks.

Thanks to Robert Ray, Bonnie Dalton, and Esther Wilson for editing and proofreading.

Thanks to my Focus Group: Pastor Germaine Wright, Clossie Ray, Lee Thompson, Gerri Holbert, Elzina Massey, Anne Wanta, Nancy Anderson, and, Lyndle Motley.

My hope is that each reader will benefit by the decisions expressed. This is my contribution to you to help in some way when decisions are difficult to make.

Sincerely,

Faye Saxon Horton

Table of Contents

Faye Saxon Horton

Introduction

Decision is defined as a conclusion or resolution made after consideration; the act of making up one's mind; firmness of purpose of character, determination. We are exploring decisions made BC (before Christ) with the impact of Decisions of Life today.

The Book of Esther is one of two Books of the Bible named after women, the other being the Book of Ruth. Women played vital roles in biblical history, if only to an extent. You may recall it was a woman, Rahab, who hid Joshua's soldiers. This decision of kindness led to freedom for Rahab and her family. Certainly you will remember the story of the Samaritan woman at the well, who by deciding to give a drink to Jesus advanced God's plan for integration? We all remember that women were the first to receive a sign of Jesus' resurrection? And, therefore, we are reminded that as women made the decision to report the good news of the resurrection of Jesus, women might be considered the first telegraph.

Esther's story is a powerful story of God's way of deliverance for His people. God had chosen, once again, to use a woman to perform a stellar task, well beyond what might have been expected at the time. The personal strength, fortitude, determination, calculated consideration, faith, and understanding required during those times is not beyond the reach of women today. This book will help us to not only learn about Queen Esther, but, the people around her, the influences of her life, as a parallel for Decisions of Life today.

God's name is not mentioned in the recording of The Book of Esther. However, Hadassah (Esther's former name) is given instructions and guidance in each phase of her journey in life. God's Hand guides Esther directly and indirectly, through her cousin, Mordecai. Throughout the Book of Esther you will be able to see the work of God through the events as they unfold. Moreover, your thoughts of today's world and relationships with family, people who serve us, people we serve, and, others may be guided by the principles used in the Book of Esther.

Faye Saxon Horton

The complete story of Queen Esther tells how the Israelites were rescued by her bravery. The decisions made to get to the desired end result, are ones we can use today.

The Book of Esther is a short read (10 chapters). May I suggest you read the Book in its entirety before or while digesting Decisions of Life. Enjoy. Let me hear from you. Send your comments to: hortoninternationalministries@gmail.com. Be ready for the next book about decisions based on The Book of Ruth. I look forward to hearing from you.

Decision 1: Do the Right Thing

"In any moment of decision the best thing you can do is the right thing, the next best thing is the wrong thing, and, the worst thing you can do is nothing."

Theodore Roosevelt (1858-1919)

Queen Esther is the heroine of this book of the Bible, however, there are two other women involved in this book. They are Queen Vashti and Zeresh, wife of Haman. The actions of each of these women will play roles in demonstrating decisions for living. Let's start at the beginning of the story, with Queen Vashti.

King Xerxes (also known as King Ahasuerus) ruled over 127 provinces from India to Ethiopia. Provinces, as you suspected, are regions separated by some geographic boundaries. Think of the vastness of King Xerxes' rule as being 127 "states", rather than 50 as in the United States. The land area might be about two and one-half times the size of the United States. The royal throne of King Xerxes was in Susa.

King Xerxes was a rich King who shared the vastness of his wealth by celebrating with his court men. The guests at the King's celebration included princes, noblemen, officials of the court, and, military leaders. This "house party" at the palace continued for 180 days (six months). When this party was over, the King ordered another party, which lasted seven days. This party was for all of the people of Susa. Each guest drank liberally, as there were no restrictions. There were no two-drinks limit, no one-drink ticket. At this party everyone was allowed to drink as much as they pleased. The King's guests were all men.

During the King's celebration, Queen Vashti held a banquet for the women in the royal palace. Scripture doesn't tell us how long Queen Vashti's girl's night out party continued, however, we might certainly say this was no seven day or six month event. After all, just as in today's times, someone needed to tend the children, run the household administratively, and, be sure everything was in order as the King wished. Queen Vashti, as well as the other women of the palace, was required to be ready and available when the King called.

On the seventh day of King Xerxes' party, King Xerxes ordered Queen Vashti to his presence to display her beauty before the men. King Xerxes asked that Queen Vashti present herself wearing her crown.

Queen Vashti refused to appear before the King, wearing her crown. Having been in the Court, and, having been Queen for some time, Queen Vashti understood the possible recoil of her actions. The Queen's decision to not present herself before hundreds of men, who by this time may have been drunk with wine, was a challenge to the laws and basic rules of the court.

Decision 1: Do the Right Thing

In today's living, women must make decisions that are contrary to the obvious. Daily there are decisions to be made that will complicate your life. The choices you make may have a lasting effect. Follow the urgings of the Holy Spirit to always Do the Right Thing, regardless the consequences. Esther would never have become Queen Esther had Queen Vashti not made the decision at this point to Do the Right Thing.

Many of us have heard the words, "Do the Right Thing."

- This is the phrase that rings in your ear when you are facing an issue or a complex decision.
- This phrase resonates with you as you decide which direction to take that may help or harm yourself or others.
- This is the phrase that your mother told you when you needed to choose to share with your friends.
- This is the phrase you hear deep inside when you need to tell something you know that should be revealed.

- This is the phrase that you hear within your heart, when you need to decide to stay in an abusive relationship or go.
- This is the phrase you hear in your heart, when you decide if your virtues are threatened.

What does doing the right thing mean to you?

Decision 2:   Prepare For the Best

"Proper Planning Prevents Poor Performance."

Unknown

Queen Vashti was dethroned for not obeying the request of King Xerxes. While she may not have been casted from the palace grounds, she was stripped of her title of Queen. Former Queen Vashti was never to appear before the King again. The seven court counsellors to the King felt that if other women were to follow the conduct of Queen Vashti and disobey the requests of their husbands, this would create havoc in their home lives and disrupt their way of living. The resolve and advice given to King Xerxes was to issue a royal decree, which could not be repealed, that each man was ruler over his own house. In other words, what the man said was what it would be.

King Xerxes, remembering he now does not have a Queen, is told by his personal attendants to begin a search throughout the kingdom for a new queen. Young, beautiful girls from all the provinces of Susa were summoned to meet with Hegai, the keeper of the King's concubines, for proper training, cleansing, purification, and selection to be presented to the King. From these women, King Xerxes would choose a new queen.

Hadassah, a beautiful, young virgin girl is about to make the biggest career decision of her life. Hadassah is who we now know as Esther. She is a morally ethic Jewish girl raised by Mordecai, her cousin. Mordecai assumed the role of mother and father for Esther after the loss of both her parents. Esther was raised in the customs of her people, and, is instructed by Mordecai not to reveal her ethnicity.

Esther arrives at the palace in Susa with the attributes that would be recognized as beautiful.

- A beautiful appearance
- Lovely eyes
- Excellent facial tone and structure
- Shapely body
- Radiant skin and complexion
- Speaks softly and kindly
- Walks with grace and confidence
- Endearing smile

Hegai sees something special in Esther when she arrives. No doubt, Hegai can see in comparison to the other women he must train, Esther, has a greater depth of beauty. Having the faith of God within and, living by the principles of her religion clearly helped Esther to have infinite beauty.

She has beauty that goes beyond skin deep, more than can be seen with the naked eye. Esther has that inner peace that shines through her very presence, because she has God. Hegai shows preferential treatment by providing Esther with special foods and supplements to further enhance her beauty in preparation of meeting the King. Esther and her maids, who were hand selected by Hegai to serve her, were moved to a special place in the palace. This preparation process took 12 months, an entire year.

The year of preparation was a complete beauty regimen, which included salts baths, fragrances, incenses, skin softeners and purifiers, special creams and lotions to enhance Esther's beauty. Today this would mean being lavishly treated with the top brand skin care products, such as Chanel, Lancome, Estee Lauder, Clinique, Revlon to mention a few. Some of the top quality fragrances might be Dior, Dolce & Gabbana, Versace, Prada, and, Gucci. You get the picture. Good quality products being used for this elaborate beauty enhancement.

During this year, I would also believe that Esther received coaching on conduct before the King, what was appropriate within the palace and what was not, how to conduct herself with the maids who attended her, how to conduct herself with the other young ladies who wanted to become queen. The time and effort put in here was all a part of a preparation to become something more.

Decision 2: Prepare For the Best

Esther was in preparation all of her life for something big to happen. Little did she know that when she was summoned to go to the palace by Mordecai that she would be God's star in the deliverance of His people. God has a plan for everyone. "For I know the plans I have for you, declares the LORD, plans to prosper you and not to harm you, plans to give you hope and a future". Jeremiah 29:11. Accept God's word as your guide, and, always prepare for the best.

Esther's decision to be mindful and respectful of Mordecai, her guardian, prepared her for what was to come. As a young girl, Esther, may not have felt she was destined for something great. In today's living, we might recognize that being without parents was never a barrier to Esther as she prepared for the best. Esther's obedience and faith endured.

What does it take for you to Prepare for the Best?

- Be forever faithful to God.

- Be expectant that the best is yet to come.

- Be mindful that God always has our best interest in His plan.

- Look for the positive in everything, everyone, and in every way.

- Live in expectancy daily.

- Consider the best for everyone around you.

- Thank God daily for the thoughts He has for you.

Decision 3: Love the Life You Live

"There are two (2) primary choices in life: to accept conditions as they exist, or accept the responsibility for changing them." Denis Watley

The process of Esther's life and growing is a curious study of servitude, love, aggressiveness intertwined with humility, permissiveness, obedience without grumbling and complaining. Esther, an orphan, raised and adopted by her cousin, Mordecai, listens and obeys instructions carefully. Not revealing her ethnicity, this young lady brings to the kingdom of Susa the strength, courage, determination, and faith necessary to survive.

At this point, Esther may be unaware of the power position she will have. She is placed in a harem of women, who all have their eyes on pleasing the King, perhaps at the costs of premarital sexual relations. Some Rabbis believe when Hegai places Esther in a special place, with special maids, her virginity is being guarded for as long as possible. Jewish law was clear about the consequences of sin against those laws.

From her humble beginnings, Esther has learned to ask for nothing more than is necessary for her at the time. She takes no more than what is given and suggested to her from Hegai as she enters the King's palace on her initial visit. Demonstrating the inner beauty and gleaming with the outer beauty that has been bestowed upon her, Esther quickly catches King Xerxes' eye. As was custom, ladies who were brought into the palace would not return, unless the King recalled them by name. It seems Esther was well remembered by the King, as she was summoned to return to the palace, where she was crowned as Queen Esther.

Decision 3: Love the Life You Live

Esther is a young lady, among thousands of others who seek approval from the King. Many of the thousands may be chosen to return to the King's palace. Only one will be chosen Queen.

Faye Saxon Horton

Decisions of Life

Esther: A young lady moving into a strange land.

Today: An eviction or removal from home or apartment.

Decision: Create comfort where you are. Focus on the beauty of living. Look for those positives that exist. Keep your home clean and orderly. Keep yourself clean and humble.

Esther: Young lady away from her heritage.

Today: Living outside of your family circle, away from sisters, brothers, aunts, uncles, cousins, nieces, nephews.

Decision: Attend church services. Visit with seniors or others with whom you may develop a familial relationship. Love others as you would yourself.

Esther: Young lady of different ethnicity.

Today: You are living among people of various backgrounds, religions, creeds, and nationalities, people with different opinions.

Decision: Admire and create understanding with others. Enjoy diversity. Learn about other cultures. Share your culture and beliefs.

Esther: Young lady without parents.

Today: No living relatives. No parental guidance. Without elder support.

Decision: Lean heavily on your faith. Develop friendships. Be a friend. Live with your heavenly Father daily.

Esther: Young lady who lives a modest life.

Today: Your financial life is in turmoil. You live paycheck to paycheck. You have more month than money.

Decision: Prioritize spending. Seek budget cutting and costs saving means of living. Develop a plan to become debt free. Ask for help. Pray for guidance.

Esther: Young lady who has infinite beauty.

Today: You have a sweet spirit. Life has been unkind.

Decision: Continue to smile. A smile will wipe away many tears. You smile and someone will smile back. Smiling is beauty and love shown on your face.

Esther: Young lady who has no profession.

Today: Undereducated or uneducated. Limited skills.

Decision: Develop the skills you have. Retrain. Seek the education you need. Improve on the skills you have. Seek ways to identify your skills.

Esther: Young lady who must keep a secret identity

Today: Secrets of your past are with you. There may be abusive relationships in your past.

Decision: Open your heart to God. Share your secret thoughts and feelings with Him. He knows. He cares. He will guide you.

Faye Saxon Horton

Decision 4: Be Ready to Serve

"Those who are happiest are those who do the most for others."
Booker T. Washington

The former Hadassah, is now Queen Esther. She has established residency in the kingdom. She is the First Lady. Queen Esther is the chief wife of the King. She is the ruler of the Ladies-in-waiting, and, the #1 choice of King Xerxes. Being appointed Queen would, by definition, make Esther the prominent woman of the Kingdom. Queen Esther now holds the place of the former Queen Vashti.

To celebrate Queen Esther, the King throws a banquet in her honor for all the nobles and officials of the court. Lavish gifts are given to people of the kingdom, as King Xerxes has considerable wealth. This celebration has a two-fold purpose. This is the wedding celebration and announcement of a new Queen. The King has complied with the counselors' suggestions to get a new Queen from among virgins of the land. King Xerxes is restored to power and favor with the people once again. King Xerxes has also satisfied his own desires with the most beautiful, hand-picked, and, groomed virgin among them all.

Mordecai continues to be a family protector providing parental guidance to Queen Esther. God has positioned Mordecai at the gates of the kingdom where many activities of the day occur. This is where everyone or anyone who wishes an audience with the King must wait until called into his presence. Mordecai's main purpose of being there is because God has positioned him there for a reason, yet to be disclosed. It is not believed that Mordecai had any wares to sell to the king, or wished to demonstrate some artistic talent before the king, or had any specific reason for an audience with the King. Mordecai is still guarding Queen Esther's life.

While outside the main gates Mordecai overhears Bigthan and Teresh plotting to kill the King. Mordecai relays this information to Queen Esther, who shares the information with the king. Naturally, Queen Esther gave her source of information and credited Mordecai with bringing this to her attention. The King's investigation determined indeed Bigthan and Teresh conspired to kill him, so they were immediately hanged.

Faye Saxon Horton

Decision 4: Be Ready to Serve

Being Ready to Serve means being attentive. Webster's definition of attentive is:

Thinking about or watching something carefully.

Paying careful attention to something.

Most concerned about the needs of others.

This Decision of Life includes paying close attention to, being closely aligned with and carefully listening to God's directions. Being attentive means living the life and making life decisions based on careful consideration of what is happening around us and in our lives. Being attentive also means heeding the word of God, listening for the inner voice that guides you. Being attentive means being ready to serve and help others, looking and listening for the opportunity to serve others. Being attentive to serving others before ourselves is God's intent and direction for our lives.

Positioned at the gate enabled Mordecai to look, listen and learn. It enabled Mordecai to serve. He watched carefully to observe what was happening around him. Mordecai paid careful attention to what he heard, and, he relayed the message to Queen Esther because of his concern for the king. Mordecai was ready to serve. Queen Esther shows her wiliness to serve by immediately informing the King of the threats to his life.

Being ready to serve, places you in a position to be ready for action to help in God's work. When we serve others, we are serving God. Putting ourselves last and others first is service to the one ultimate Servant, Jesus Christ. To be a true servant and ready for service means that we will do all that Jesus asks us to do.

We have a niece in Jacksonville, Florida who always sees beauty in others. After observing her in the presence of others, her way of attentively serving is to offer kind compliments. Our niece's words have been uplifting to others when she least expects. She is actually serving through her ministry of compliments. God bless you, Niece.

These are examples of decisions to serve:

- Cook dinner for a senior neighbor.
- Ask if you can get something from the store for a neighbor who has no car, or who may be sick.
- Give a smile to everyone.
- Share a compliment with strangers.
- Give a portion of what you have to someone who needs.
- Observe the Sabbath, serve at your church or worship place.
- Volunteer to help whenever possible, wherever possible.
- When you see a need for service, step up and volunteer to do without being asked.
- Look around for the needs of others.
- Share your talent with others.
- Speak a kind and encouraging word to someone who appears distressed.

- Use what you have to help others.
- Bless the ones around you with your wisdom and knowledge.
- When invited for a meal, help with the clean-up.
- Volunteer to prepare a meal for someone who needs it.
- Deliver the goodness and mercies God gives to you to others.
- Take a youth to a play, a sports event, a concert, a cultural event.
- Open your heart, mind and hands to others.
- Listen for the needs of others.
- Give generously and liberally to others.
- Ask for guidance in helping others daily.
- Renew friendships.
- Offer sincere compliments.

Decision 5: Worship God Only

"Thou shalt not bow down thyself to them, nor serve them...."
Exodus 20:5 KJV

Haman, the Agagite, one of the most prominent princes in the region, was granted special honors by King Xerxes. Haman was given a seat of honor above the other nobles. These honors required that everyone bow before Haman when in his presence. Everyone at the gates to the kingdom knelt and gave honor to Haman, except Mordecai. Day after day, Mordecai refused to bow to Haman. Frustrated with such sedition, the officials at the gate asked why?

Mordecai's answer was simple. Being a believer in God and a follower of God's laws, he could not bow before Haman. God's first commandment is "You shall have no other gods before me." Exodus 20:3. Now put yourselves in Haman's shoes. Haman feels totally embarrassed, shamed, red-faced, bewildered, humiliated, dishonored, and, wants to seek revenge. Haman's anger from this situation spawned a desire to not only kill Mordecai, but to destroy the Jews throughout the kingdom.

Daily living requires that we obey God's commandments, starting with the first commandment. God has given the laws He requires. He requires holiness and the utmost praise and worship only to God Almighty. A decision to worship God requires that we not allow anything to become more important to us than God. God is God.

Mordecai respected Haman, as another man. However, he honored God not Haman. Mordecai respected Haman in his position of authority; however, he felt strongly to bow before Haman was a form of worship. No doubt Mordecai saw this as placing Haman on a pedestal above God Almighty. Mordecai demonstrated his faith and belief in the ordinances of his religion, although it meant disfavor from Haman and the officials of the kingdom. This is the type respectfulness God requires.

Decision 5: Worship God Only

In today's living, we are often tested to "bow down" to other gods. Women are tested daily with how we look, how we dress, what to wear, how we interact with others, how we gain acceptance, how we feel about ourselves, how we learn, what we learn, how we live, where we live, how we speak, when to speak, how we interact with others, with whom we should interact, and, the list goes on. Temptations to care more about money, looks, possessions, clothes and ourselves loom around us daily. As Mordecai, we must remember that God is the Almighty God, and, He only should we worship. There should be nothing we value or praise above God.

Decision 6: Keep a Positive and Open Mind

"If you cannot be open-minded, then you do not possess your ideas, your ideas possess you."
Bryant McGill

Haman has now become obsessed with the fact that Mordecai does not honor or worship him. Haman   is so focused on revenge against Mordecai that he closes his mind and heart to options. The decision Haman made with a closed mind was to destroy Mordecai and all his people. Haman deceives King Xerxes by persuading him that there is a group of people in the kingdom who live by different laws and do not obey the laws of the King. King Xerxes issued an edict condemning all Jews to death.

Decision 6: Keep a Positive and Open Mind

You may ask, why is it an important decision to Keep a Positive and Open Mind? If your mind is not open to the word of God and his instructions, then your heart is not open to doing the right thing, preparing for excellency, serving others, and living in peace.

Your mind works continually. Thoughts are always present. Keeping a positive and open mind requires you to listen for options, consider alternatives, seek advice and counsel, research the reasons you are faced with a decision, look at all sides, consider the possibilities, review the pros and cons. Keeping an open mind also means asking for God's guidance, and making decisions based on the "big" picture, not merely your personal concerns.

To have a positive mind allows you to make decisions based on the righteousness of God. Consider that there are a minimum of two options in every decision:

- yes or no
- right or wrong
- good or evil
- positive or negative
- better or worse
- good or bad
- likely or less likely
- forward or backward
- moving or status quo

There may be more than two options, however, if you focus on but one, as Haman, you have locked out other possibilities for reaching an amicable agreement, settling a situation, or changing your thinking. This brings us to the fact that an open and positive mind allows for learning. Learning allows for more wisdom and knowledge. Additional knowledge about any situation increases the strength of an opinion.

Decision 7: Pray Always

"Prayer is not asking. Prayer is putting oneself in the hands of God, at His disposition, and listening to His voice in the depth of our hearts."

Mother Teresa

When Mordecai learns of Haman's plot to have all Jews killed, he is distraught. Mordecai covers himself in sackcloth and ashes, significant at the time of a person who is grieving. As word spread throughout Susa, many Jews covered themselves in sackcloth and ashes, while wailing and crying loudly. Queen Esther receives the report of Mordecai's behavior, and, wants to know immediately why her cousin is acting in this manner. Although Queen Esther sends clothing to Mordecai, he refuses to wear the garments sent for his use.

Hatach is sent to speak with Mordecai. Mordecai sends back a report to the Queen that Haman, through King Xerxes, has plotted legally to kill all the Jews. At this point, Mordecai asks Queen Esther to go into the King to intercede for the Jews, her people.

Faye Saxon Horton

Queen Esther is somewhat surprised at this request, as Mordecai is aware that no one enters the King's court without his express invitation. Should Queen Esther enter the King's court, and, the King does not extend his hand to her, she would be put to death. Mordecai reminds Queen Esther of her ethnicity, which means should all Jews die, she would be included. *"For if you remain silent at this time, relief and deliverance for the Jews will arise from another place, but you and your father's family will perish. And who knows but that you have come to royal position for such a time as this?" Esther 4:14*

Queen Esther is now faced with a decision to appear before the king without permission. This decision might be bolder than the decision of Queen Vashti to not appear before the King when summoned. Before Queen Esther goes before the King, she asks all the Jews to fast and pray, along with her, her maidens and servants, for three days. After the three day fast she boldly enters the court.

Decision 7: Pray Always

Prayer is an integral part of life. Prayer must be an integral part of decisions we make today. Actually, no decision should be made without prayer. *"Pray continually". I Thessalonians 5:17.* It seems Queen Esther asked for fasting and prayer because she was faced with a life or death situation. We should not wait for a life or death situation to pray. Prayer is closeness to God. Prayer brings us to those right decisions of life. Prayer can be a simple sentence or request of God. Pray with faith and believing in your prayers.

ALWAYS
Pray
And
Never give up
LUKE 18:1

One sentence prayers for today's decisions:

- Thank you Lord for keeping me safe.
- Dear Lord, guide me today.
- Our Father, bless the poor.
- Lord, give me the strength to get through this day.
- Heavenly Father, thanks that your will is for my good.
- Oh Lord, guide my tongue as I make request for a raise.
- Bless me indeed, increase my territory. Thank you, Lord.
- Lord, I pray health and healing for the sick of the world.
- Lord, provide me with the guidance to do your will.
- Our Father, keep my mind and heart open to do your will.
- Dear Lord, help me to seek you.
- Father, bless my children.
- Lord, thank you for the good grades from my children.
- Dear God, thank you for employment.
- Help me to be the person you would have me to be.
- Thanks for your more than enough blessings.
- Lord, thanks for health and happiness.
- Thank you Lord, for waking me up today.
- Thank you for a blessed day.
- Dear God, help me to help someone today.
- Thank you, Holy Spirit.

Decision 8: Set Goals with God

"... a man plans his course, but the LORD determines his steps."

Proverbs 16:9

On the third day, Queen Esther enters the inner court of the palace. The King extends the gold scepter to her, without hesitation, and she enters. Naturally, the King wants to know why Queen Esther has risked her life to see him unannounced. The King so moved by Queen Esther's appearance, says he will grant her up to one-half of the kingdom, if she so desires. Queen Esther requests, if it pleases the King, that he would come to a banquet she has prepared for him. The Queen further invites Haman, who King Xerxes has promoted to the highest noble position, to dine with them.

King Xerxes called for Haman right away to go with him to the feast Queen Esther has prepared. As they are drinking wine and eating lavishly, the King once again asks the Queen for her request. Realizing the severity of Queen Esther's unannounced entrance into the palace, King Xerxes no doubt suspects she has an agenda, a goal, a plan, or a big request. What might she want from the King that would be so important for her to risk her life?

Queen Esther gives the King her petition and request. It is simply that if King Xerxes and Haman will come tomorrow to a banquet she prepares she will answer the King's question and reveal her wishes.

Haman leaves the first luncheon in great spirits, rushing home to boast to his friends and wife, Zeresh, about the position he now has in the kingdom. Haman has received great favor from King Xerxes. Haman reports that he is the only person invited to lunch with Queen Esther and the King. Furthermore, Haman is the only person invited the next day to dine with Queen Esther and the King Xerxes.

Haman is just not satisfied with these honors and privileges, although he is happy about them. Bothered by the continuing one thought, revenge on Mordecai, Haman is not completely a happy man. Zeresh suggests Haman should erect a pole reaching about 75 feet, and ask the King's permission to hang Mordecai the next day. Zeresh does not consult with anyone, but encourages Haman in his quest to remove Mordecai once and for all. By focusing on the one desire of Haman, to kill all Jews, Zeresh misses the opportunity to play a key role in the direction of Haman's career and his life.

In the meantime, the King goes back to the palace and cannot rest. As sleep evades the King, he starts to read the book of his reign. King Xerxes finds the recording that Mordecai exposed Bigthana and Teresh, two of the king's officers who were conspiring to assassinate the king. No honor or recognition had been given to Mordecai for this discovery. As Haman enters the court to ask King Xerxes about hanging Mordecai, the King asks Haman what honor might be given to a man the king wishes to delight.

Haman assumes the man to be honored must surely be himself. His suggestion to the King was to allow one of the nobles to cloth the man in a royal robe the King has worn, place the man on a royal horse with the royal crest, and proclaim throughout the streets, this is how the King honors one who delights the King. Surprisingly, King Xerxes instructs Haman to personally carry out all the suggestions he has given with Mordecai.

Haman's goal was to exalt himself before the King and all the people of Susa. Zeresh's goal was to please her husband. God's plan was to provide Mordecai with the honor and praise he deserved for obeying God's will.

Decision 8: Set Goals with God

Ours is a goal oriented society. It is believed that once goals are set, everything humanly possible should be done to meet those goals. In business and in your careers, goals are often set for you. Goals should be attainable, realistic, measurable, identifiable, and are associated with a timeline. Trust in God to prepare you to set goals that have these characteristics, on God's timeline.

Seek wise counsel when planning and setting goals. "Plans fail for lack of counsel, but with many advisers they succeed". Proverbs 15:22

Put your plans and goals in God's hands. "Therefore do not worry about tomorrow, for tomorrow will worry about itself. Each day has enough trouble of its own." Matthew 6:34

Make careful planning throughout life. "Now listen, you who say, 'Today or tomorrow we will go to this or that city, spend a year there, carry on business and make money.' Why, you do not even know what will happen tomorrow. What is your life? You are a mist that appears for a little while and then vanishes. Instead, you ought to say, 'if it is the Lord's will, we will live and do this or that.' As it is, you boast and brag. All such boasting is evil. Anyone, then, who knows the good he ought to do and doesn't do it sins." James 4:13-16

Decision 9: Trust God

"Trust in the Lord with all your heart, and do not lean on your own understanding. In all your ways acknowledge Him, and He will make your paths straight."

Proverbs 3:5-6

Queen Esther has asked all the Jews to fast and pray for three days. She now places all her trust in God to go before her, guide her and direct the outcomes of her actions.

Queen Esther asks King Xerxes and Haman to come to a banquet she prepared. During lunch at the first request of Queen Esther, King Xerxes and Haman attend, and are served well. Queen Esther asks that the King and Haman come to lunch again the next day, and, she will reveal her request. When asked at the second luncheon, what is her request, Queen Esther tells her Majesty, the King, her petition is that her life and the lives of her people will be spared. Queen Esther goes on to explain that their lives have been sold for the purpose of killing all of them.

Queen Esther is precious to the King. He is quite surprised that someone would want to kill his Queen, his bride, his love, and all her people. King Xerxes leaves the luncheon enraged when he learned the perpetrator is Haman.

Haman stays with Queen Esther to plead for mercy, and, lies on the couch where Queen Esther is reclining. As the King returns, he sees Haman in this position, and, immediately orders that Haman is hanged on the gallows he has set up to hang Mordecai.

Decision 9: Trust in God

The decision to Trust in God may be easier said than done. It takes extraordinary courage to speak up for your beliefs and be willing to suffer the consequences when your beliefs are against tradition. God's people are called for a purpose. God's people are prepared by God to be used for his purpose.

Queen Esther's decision to speak up for her life and her people was tremendously courageous. However, utilizing the precursor of fasting and praying, she was shored up to do this big task. Queen Esther was at the point of her destiny. She discovered her purpose and how to carry it out. Both the discovery and the action plan were done with immense Trust in God.

Build trust daily. Build trust in God in small ways. Add to your trust daily. Take small steps, then bigger steps. Seek God's guidance. Leave the outcomes to Him. Enjoy the peace of understanding that "God's got this."

Decision 10: Choose the first 9 Decisions

"Don't fear failure so much that you refuse to try new things. The saddest summary of a life contains three descriptions: could have, might have, and should have."

Louis E. Boone

Here is the bottom line. Decisions of Life are decisions you will face several times each day. For some of us, these decisions will come easily, as you may live and practice making decisions the way this book suggests. For others, some slight or even greater changes may be necessary in your daily lives. The main focus is on the scriptures referenced in this book. Embrace Change.

Here is a revelation for you. I have always considered myself to be fairly intelligent. After all, I graduated Suma Cum Laude, made the Dean's list, Honor Roll student, quick to learn concepts and basics. Just this year, I have come to fully realize that none of those accomplishments were mine. God has directed my steps from birth. I give Him all the credit and the praise. I am thankful that God has guided me to where I am and will continue to guide me.

Let's review those nine (9) Decisions of Life:

1. Do the Right Thing

Do the Right Thing when it seems contrary to what others think. Do the Right Thing when it seems contrary to what you think. Do the Right Thing just because it is the Right Thing.

2. Prepare For the Best

Prepare yourself mentally, physically, emotionally, and, spiritually for living the best life. If you don't know or have not experienced a better life, ask God's guidance in what is the best life for you.

3. Love the Life you Live

Wherever you are in life make it the best until you can move to a higher level. Use all the resources God has provided to love where you are. Learn from the experience where you are. Learn how to use what you have to get you to where you want to be.

4. Be Ready to Serve

Loving and serving is what we are destined to do. Jesus loved and served us by giving his life for us. What better way to serve Him than to serve others? Look for ways to help, serve, minister and love others.

5. Worship God Only

God is a jealous God. God has an immense store of resources, all for you. He asks that you worship Him above all others. Set aside your Holy Day. Observe the Sabbath, with praise and worship to God. Throughout the week, let nothing be more important than your time with God.

6. Keep a Positive and Open Mind

Unlimited opportunity will be revealed when you can rise above the "fray". Stay above the gossip, backbiting, tattling, carrying ill messages, and, living in constant communications with others who do the same. A positive and open mind is a mind that thinks like God.

7. Pray Always

We are often trained to pray before bedtime and at mealtime. We learn it is important to pray first thing in the morning. There is no appointment needed with God to pray. Pray always and continuously. Pray about everything. Pray silently. Pray openly. Pray alone. Pray with others. Pray without ceasing.

8. Set Goals With God

As I now realize, there is nothing I can do without God. God is my Creator, my Father and He will be with me on every journey towards the goals that I set. We must remember God's plan for us is not our plan. God's plan for us is far larger and better than any plan we can imagine. So, set goals with God.

9. Trust in God

Understand and believe that there is an Almighty God. Believe and trust that He has you in his heart. Know and trust that God will take care of you, no matter what your shortcomings. Trust and believe.

It's now up to you!

Decision 11: Celebrate God's Goodness

"The blessing of the Lord makes rich, and he adds no sorrow ...."
Proverbs 10:22

This is a list of the rewards to Queen Esther and Mordecai for faithfully following God's plan for them.

1. Queen Esther received the estate of Haman.
2. Mordecai was given the King's signet ring.
3. Mordecai was appointed, by Queen Esther, to be in charge of Haman's estate.
4. A decree went out reversing Haman's order to kill the Jews.
5. Mordecai writes the rescinding decree and seals it with the signet ring.
6. Jews in every city were given authority to defend themselves.
7. Jews were triumphant in battle against their enemies.
8. Mordecai was promoted in the King's palace.
9. The Festival of Purim was established and is continued today.

When God makes us rich with His blessings, there is cause to celebrate. Truly, if we are remembering and giving praise with thanksgiving, we would have a celebration every day. Let us always celebrate God's goodness, as we are full of his richness.

Make Decisions of Life that will bring you into the goodness of God!

ABOUT THE AUTHOR

Faye Saxon Horton was born in Winter Haven, Florida and graduated Suma Cum Laude from Albertus Magnus College with a degree in Business Management. She is the author of "How to Start a Maid Service".

Her professional career spans 30+ years in the insurance industry; working for Aetna, Anthem Blue Cross/Blue Shield, Colonial and Humana. Faye has served as Employee Benefits Officer at the former New Haven Savings Bank, New Haven, CT, and member of Board of Directors of Connecticare Health Insurance Company, Farmington, CT.

In addition to golf, Faye enjoys reading, sewing, travelling and helping others. She is the wife of Norris Horton, retired State Marshall, Past President of United Golfers Association, Life member and past President of Knickerbocker Golf Club.

Norris and Faye attend Covenant Love Christian Center, North Richland Hills, TX and New Covenant Baptist Church, Orlando, FL.

www.ingramcontent.com/pod-product-compliance
Lightning Source LLC
Chambersburg PA
CBHW071743020426
42331CB00008B/2150